HOW TO BUILD A CONVENIENCE STORE BUSINESS

Build a Business Collection

By

TK Johnson

Digital Edition V 1.0

Copyright 2015 by Build a Business Collection

All rights reserved. No part of this book may be reproduced by any means whatsoever without the written permission from the author, except brief portions quoted for purpose of review.

Re-selling through electronic outlets (like Amazon, Barnes and Nobles or E-bay) without permission of the publisher is illegal and punishable by law.

The scanning, uploading, and distribution of this book via the Internet or via any other means without the permission of the publisher is illegal and punishable by law.

Please purchase only authorized editions and do not participate in or encourage electronic piracy of copyrightable materials.

Your support of the author's right is appreciated.

All information in this book has been carefully researched and checked for factual accuracy. However, the author and publisher make no warranty, express or implied, that the information contained herein is appropriate for every individual, situation, or purpose, and assumes no responsibility for errors or omissions. The reader assumes the risk and responsibility for all actions, and the author will not be held responsible for any loss or damage, whether consequential, incidental, and special or otherwise that may result from the information presented in this publication.

I have relied on my own experience as well as many different sources for this book, and I have done my best to check facts and to give credit where it is due. In the event that any material is incorrect or has been used without proper permission please contact me so that the oversight can be corrected.

Build a Business Collection

info@buildabusinessbooks.com

Contents

Introduction 6
Overview of Industry 8
Daily Duties 11
Negatives 13
Overhead 17
Which type of business should I setup? 20
Where to set up your business? 27
Accountants and Lawyers 30
Business Cards and Websites 32
Employees 35
Interview Process 40
Personality Tests 44
Payroll 46
Average Salaries 47
Job Ads 48
Systems 52
Productized Services 56
Location 60
Healthcare 64
Requirements 67
Taxes 71

Expenses	73
Audits	78
Marketing	81
Networking	87
Seminars & Conferences	91
Linkedin Pages	92
Other Networking Opportunities	93
Profit	94
Margins	97
Public Relations	105
Customer Management	108
Additional Resources	110
MASTERMINDS	112

Introduction

I'll keep it short and sweet. This book will give you very good overview of what you will need to start and succeed in your business.

There are different ways of reading these types of books but here is the best way to read this one.

Quickly skim through it and look through the chapters. If an idea grabs you go with it and dig deeper down that rabbit hole. (Listen to the podcast if there's one on that particular topic.)

You want to keep being excited as this will be a long road.

Once you're done then get back to the beginning.

Read through the book quickly.

Read again and take notes.

Listen to the rest of the podcasts and grab your [free resources](). There's a chapter at the end with another link to those so no worries... you will not miss it.

*Leadership is a potent combination of strategy and character.
But if you must be without one, be without the strategy.*

Norman Schwarzkopf

A meeting is an event at which the minutes are kept and the hours are lost.

Unknown

You are not your resume, you are your work.

Seth Godin

Beware of any enterprise requiring new clothes.

Henry Thoreau

One finds limits by pushing them.

Herbert Simon

If you see a bandwagon, it's too late.

James Goldsmith

Overview of Industry

A convenience store is like a mini supermarket. There are plenty of these stores all around the country and has proven to be very helpful to people especially to those who are on the road. It was in 1927 when the first convenience store established in the US in Dallas, Texas. Since then 7-11 along with other convenience store grew over time. Today these companies are among the billion earners in the industry. It's not surprising to see that there are plenty of people who are investing in this type of business with the hopes of one day making an empire for themselves just like the pioneers in this business.

With an increase of 11% in the jobs in this industry, there is a good chance that convenient stores will continue to flourish over the next decade. Investing in this business today will prove to be profitable in the future.

Business opportunities are like buses, there's always another one coming.
Richard Branson

You must be the change you wish to see in the world.
Mahatma Gandhi

You only have to do a very few things right in your life so long as you don't do too many things wrong.
Warren Buffett

The trick is in what one emphasizes. We either make ourselves miserable, or we make ourselves strong. The amount of work is the same.
Carlos Castaneda

There's no shortage of remarkable ideas, what's missing is the will to execute them.
Seth Godin

The great accomplishments of man have resulted from the transmission of ideas of enthusiasm.
Thomas J. Watson

Daily Duties

To know what the daily duties of a convenience store are, here are a few:

- Welcomes customers to the store.

- Offers help with the merchandise selections.

- Makes sure that the shopping carts are arranged.

- Gives information regarding the products, ingredients, nutritional value etc.

- Receives and answers calls from customers for inquiries.

- Conducts inventories of the sales and products.

- Handles complaints from customers and quickly resolves them.

- Makes sure that the store is clean and pleasing to customers.

- Removes and disposes trash.
- Checks for the stocks and makes sure that they are restocked regularly.
- Handles the cash and operates the cash register.
- Makes sure that the merchandise are in proper aisle, price, signage and code.
- Makes sure the the freezer are secured and all items that needed to be chilled or frozen are in place.
- Records inventories and makes report.
- Trains employees if needed.

Negatives

Owning and running a convenient store is a good investment. Some of the biggest stores in the country like Walmart and 7-11 started as small convenient stores but are now among the biggest earners in the US. If you are planning to invest in this type of business, it is best to know what you are getting yourself into. Identifying the negative sides to this investment can help you plan out an effective business plan. Here are some of the downsides of owning a convenient store.

- There is a risk of being robbed. There have been numerous reports of convenient stores being robbed. This cannot be avoided as there are so many people with bad intentions out there. The best thing that you can do is to protect your employees and investment by installing security systems and video surveillance.

- Part time workers don't always stay long. Most of the time you need to hire extra man power for the job. This is where part timers come in. Since they are working part time, you cannot avoid that your worker might just leave one day if they don't like working any longer.

- Employees tend to slack off. There are times when employees slack off especially if there are not much work or customers. It's important to brief your employees about this type of behavior and remind them of the consequences if they are caught slacking while working.

- Competition is present especially if there are alsready convenient stores around your area. It's best to observe your competition and take note of their tactics so you can improve your own.

- Working for 24 hours is a must. If you are trying to get back the investment you have put in, opening your store 24/7 is a good option but risky choice.

Everything should be made as simple as possible, but not simpler.

Albert Einstein

Far and away the best prize that life offers is the chance to work hard at work worth doing.

Theodore Roosevelt

Change is not a threat, it's an opportunity. Survival is not the goal, transformative success is.

Seth Godin

Even if you are on the right track, You'll get run over if you just sit there.

Will Rogers

You must either modify your dreams or magnify your skills.

Jim Rohn

Look well to this day. Yesterday is but a dream and tomorrow is only a vision. But today well lived makes every yesterday a dream of happiness and every tomorrow a vision of hope. Look well therefore to this day.

Francis Gray

Overhead

Why would I give this term its own chapter?

It is important.

It also destroys most businesses.

Very easy to allow this one to get out of control.

Overhead consists of rent, insurance, phone/internet bills, utilities, food, paper, ink, other small services, bills, charges, subscriptions, employees and everything else combined that does not look so scary when looked at individually but can add up very fast.

Keep track of it or you will regret it. Always think about how to get this down without hurting the quality of what you are selling.

Types of Overhead Costs

To truly analyze what are the true examples of overhead costs in your business ask yourself this one question: "What must I pay for each month in order to keep my business open?"

Typical overhead expenses (sometimes referred to as fixed costs) include items such as:

- Office Salaries
- Employee Benefits
- Payroll Taxes
- Advertising
- Stationery, Office Supplies & Postage
- Legal and Professional Services
- Outside Services (Performed monthly)
- Company Car Expense
- Dues & Subscriptions
- Data Processing
- Travel & Entertainment
- Rent or Mortgage
- Building Maintenance
- Interest on Loans or Mortgages
- Insurances & Taxes
- Depreciation
- Utilities

There are also overhead costs to consider if you have more than one department within your business.

Types of Overhead Costs

Departmental Overhead Costs

If you have a sales department and perhaps a shipping department, there are other examples of overhead costs to include:

- Department Specific Advertising
- Supplies
- Uniforms
- Training
- Policy Expense – This is a cost you may incur each month where a mishap occurs and you must eat the cost and should be expensed to the department where the mishap occurred.

Some businesses will include departmental wages as fixed expenses but usually only those salaries or wages that remain the same each pay period with no variation.

Which type of business should I setup?

I know you can't wait to get your hands dirty and start making money but this step is very important. You will need to decide on a business structure. We live in a country ran by lawyers and where people love to sue each other. Due to this you should separate your personal possessions from your business. If your business goes bust or someone decides to go after you because they walked into a wall and spilled a cup of coffee on themselves it will mean that you are protected and your belongings are safe.

Most magazines recommend a sole proprietorship, a partnership or an LLC (Limited Liability Company). There other types of corporations that you can setup but for a small business starting out they are an overkill so you shouldn't worry about them now. Those other types will also cause a lot of additional accounting headaches and be more expensive to maintain.

I do not recommend a sole proprietorship. This one is the easiest as you don't actually need to file anything but gives you zero protection and a 15% self-employment tax.

Partnerships are similar except that you now allow another person into your business. You may be responsible for their mistakes and your personal items are at risk. House, car, TV... you know... the small stuff.

I'm a big fan of LLCs and recommend these the most. You have a small setup and maintenance fee but you are protected from lawsuits. This type of setup also helps with taxes and allows to deduct much more. It's a basic corporation which means that in the eyes of the law it is its own person. It can buy things, earn credit and borrow money. It is not a real corporation though which means that you can issue stock options or go public and make millions from the stock market.

Remember that the initial choice does not forfeit your rights to change later on. Times change, situations change and you can make choices more beneficial to you later on when you're good and ready.

Type of Entity	Main Advantages	Main Advantages
Sole Proprietorship	Simple and inexpensive to create and operate Owner reports profit or loss on his or her personal tax return Simple and inexpensive to create and operate	Owner personally liable for business debts
General Partnership	General partners can raise cash without involving outside investors in management of business Owners have limited personal liability for business debts	General partners personally liable for business debts
Limited Partnership	Owners (partners) report their share of profit or loss on their personal tax returns Limited partners have limited personal liability for business debts as long as they don't participate in management	Owners (partners) personally liable for business debts More expensive to create than general partnership

Type of Entity	Main Advantages	Main Advantages
Regular Corporation	Fringe benefits can be deducted as business expense	More expensive to create than partnership or sole proprietorship
	Owners can split corporate profit among owners and corporation, paying lower overall tax rate	Paperwork can seem burdensome to some owners
	Owners have limited personal liability for business debts	Separate taxable entity
S Corporation	Owners report their share of corporate profit or loss on their personal tax returns	More expensive to create than partnership or sole proprietorship
	Owners can use corporate loss to offset income from other sources	More paperwork than for a limited liability company, which offers similar advantages
		Income must be allocated to owners according to their ownership interests

Type of Entity	Main Advantages	Main Advantages
Professional Corporation	Owners have no personal liability for malpractice of other owners	Fringe benefits limited for owners who own more than 2% of shares
		More expensive to create than partnership or sole proprietorship
		Paperwork can seem burdensome to some owners
		All owners must belong to the same profession
Nonprofit Corporation	Corporation doesn't pay income taxes	Full tax advantages available only to groups organized for charitable, scientific, educational, literary, or religious purposes
	Contributions to charitable corporation are tax deductible	Property transferred to corporation stays there; if corporation ends, property must go to another nonprofit

Type of Entity	Main Advantages	Main Advantages
Limited Liability Company	Fringe benefits can be deducted as business expense Owners have limited personal liability for business debts even if they participate in management	More expensive to create than partnership or sole proprietorship State laws for creating LLCs may not reflect latest federal tax changes
Professional Limited Liability Company	IRS rules now allow LLCs to choose between being taxed as partnership or corporation Same advantages as a regular limited liability company	Same as for a regular limited liability company Members must all belong to the same profession
Limited Liability Partnership	Owners (partners) aren't personally liable for the malpractice of other partners Owners report their share of profit or loss on their personal tax returns	Unlike a limited liability company or a professional limited liability company, owners (partners) remain personally liable for many types of obligations owed to business creditors, lenders, and landlords Not available in all states Often limited to a short list of professions

Where to set up your business?

If you can run your business online and I recommend you do if possible then set the company up in Wyoming. I did a lot of research on this so you're good to go. The benefits in privacy and taxes make this the right choice.

For any brick and mortar location you will need to set it up in the state that you are in.

If you are setting up a business in multiple states or live (and also do some business) in a state other than the one where you set up the original business... you might have to submit additional paperwork in that state.

Here's an example:

Let's say you setup an LLC in Illinois. You are protected and have limited liability in that state.

Your house is in Wisconsin and you have a couple of clients there. You sometimes meet with them at a coffee shop and do business in Wisconsin. You are no longer protected by the

Illinois incorporation and might be breaking some state laws of Wisconsin.

If you're going to get fancy I recommend to consult with a lawyer.

Imagination is everything. It is the preview of life's coming attractions.

Albert Einstein

Leadership is the art of getting someone else to do something you want done because he wants to do it.

Dwight Eisenhower

Never interrupt your enemy when he is making a mistake.

Napoleon Bonaparte

To be successful, you have to have your heart in your business, and your business in your heart.

Sr. Thomas Watson

Every accomplishment starts with a decision to try.

Unknown

The first one gets the oyster the second gets the shell.

Andrew Carnegie

Accountants and Lawyers

You will need a lawyer to setup your business. We talk about that in a different chapter. Everything else can wait.

It's true that it is very important to have a great lawyer and a great accountant. However, that is after you're already running a profitable business and not before. These guys are a supportive team and anything they do or touch will cost you money. That is money that you cannot afford to spend when you are first starting out and trying to grow your business.

Helpful Episode:

LISTEN HERE

buildabusinessbooks.com/ep1

Whether you think you can or whether you think you can't, you're right!

Henry Ford

A business has to be involving, it has to be fun, and it has to exercise your creative instincts.

Richard Branson

People rarely buy what they need. They buy what they want.

Seth Godin

We generate fears while we sit. We over come them by action. Fear is natures way of warning us to get busy.

Dr. Henry Link

Live daringly, boldly, fearlessly. Taste the relish to be found in competition – in having put forth the best within you.

Henry J. Kaiser

Success is often achieved by those who don't know that failure is inevitable.

Coco Chanel

Business Cards and Websites

The biggest mistake I see a lot of people doing is getting the business cards and websites done before they even sell anything or get their first client. I understand that we all want to look good, be respected and appreciated.... I really do. The problem with this approach is that in itself it does not make money. It also has you focusing on the wrong things and it costs money and time. Someone will have to design your card and your websites. As someone that has dealt with designers & web site builders for a very long time and the clients getting these done... it is a pain and always takes much longer than everyone thinks.

I'd rather spend that money buying ads (whether they're online or offline), printing out flyers or doing some type of direct mail campaign. The rest of the time should be spend making calls, knocking on doors and networking.

Once you start making money and have people asking you for a business card and/or website than go right ahead. Get them done.

A man should never neglect his family for business.

Walt Disney

Sometimes when you innovate, you make mistakes. It is best to admit them quickly and get on with improving your other innovations.

Steve Jobs

Business is more exciting than any game.

Lord Beaverbrook

The successful man is the one who finds out what is the matter with his business before his competitors do.

Roy L. Smith

The winners in life think constantly in terms of I can, I will, and I am. Losers, on the other hand, concentrate their waking thoughts on what they should have or would have done, or what they can't do.

Dennis Waitley

Work expands so as to fill the time available for its completion.

Cyril Northcote Parkinson/Parkinson's Law.

Employees

As soon as you start making any type of money in your business then you need to start getting help. This is the fastest way to become successful. Delegation and management of others does lead to the promise land.

There are a few different ways to go about this:

Partnerships – Although I am completely against partners when it comes to running a business.... this is different. It's smart to package your work with other complementary offers and work with other companies to fulfill them. When this is done correctly, it can multiply your sales and theirs as you now have multiple companies selling the same products and helping each other succeed.

Full-Time workers – This sound like a no-brainer but hold on there just for a second professor. Anytime you hire someone full time the government steps in and sets down some pretty serious rules. A lot of it also depends on the amount of full timers but just understand that you will be paying quite a bit of taxes, unemployment insurance and possibly health care. I had a coffee shop where each full time worker cost me double. Their salary and another that went to the government. The details are beyond the scope of this book but keep this in mind.

Part-Time workers – I like these. Hopefully with systems in place they are replicable. No over time for part timers and not much hassle when it comes to making changes. You will pay some taxes but don't worry about unemployment of healthcare.

Consultants – These can be helpful for some things but not recommended. Some examples of them are Accountants, Lawyers, Marketing companies, SEO companies, Web Designers, Cleaners etc. Use them only when you need to but do not rely on any too much. If the SEO Company is in charge of all your leads... you do not have a business.

Freelancers/Contractors – Good for one of jobs. If you are not a brick and mortar and can work location independent... these guys can be your "full time" and "part time" staff (but obviously don't say that out loud to anyone). This way you give them a 1099 and they are treated as a business expense. Love this.

Interns – If you can get someone to work for a pizza, a dream or a school credit... do it. Keep in mind that they do need extra training and watching over but this is where systems come in.

Outsource – You've probably heard about Virtual Staff. The workers in the Philippines, India, Romania that power most of the international companies. They are great and not as expensive as the US work force. Anything that does not need to be done face-to-face with a customer (and as long as the US law doesn't disallow it) can be outsourced. Some tasks might be under some kind of a privacy act which does not allow the information to leave your actual office. The payments are usually done via PayPal and can be treated as an expense. Also a win and a topic that is beyond the scope of this book.

Helpful Episode:

[LISTEN HERE](buildabusinessbooks.com/ep2)

buildabusinessbooks.com/ep2

I feel that luck is preparation meeting opportunity.

Oprah Winfrey

Ideas in secret die. They need light and air or they starve to death.

Seth Godin

The true entrepreneur is a doer, not a dreamer.

Unknown

My son is now an 'entrepreneur'. That's what you're called when you don't have a job.

Ted Turner

The man who will use his skill and constructive imagination to see how much he can give for a dollar, instead of how little he can give for a dollar, is bound to succeed.

Henry Ford

For all of its faults, it gives most hardworking people a chance to improve themselves economically, even as the deck is stacked in favor of the privileged few. Here are the choices most of us face in such a system: Get bitter or get busy.

Bill O' Reilly

Interview Process

Here are some tips that I've learned while hiring.

It's more important to have an honest, punctual and competent person than a skilled applicant. Obviously you will not be hiring someone that doesn't know anything for a skilled position. However, if you have a group of people applying that pass the minimum requirements then always focus on the personality rather than a fat resume and good recommendations (which can all be faked). Being late and other small negative behavior traits are a good window into the future.

The best way to find out if a person is right for the job is to have them work on something and watch how they do.

The best interview questions are open ended. Ask about opinions, why they think a certain way and what they would do in certain situations rather than about their past accomplishments and how they would describe themselves. Keep in mind that there are coaches and books that get people ready for the most common questions. If you ask the things that all other employers ask for... you will see a performance.

In your job ad make sure to put a very small detail that will show if the applicant is actually paying attention or shooting out resumes by the hundreds. Example: Please post the words 'purple rainbow' in the header of your e-mail next to your name and position you are applying for. If they can't do that much... don't expect a good employee.

Please think about your legacy, because you're writing it every day.

Gary Vaynerchuck

Victory goes to the player who makes the next-to-last mistake.

Savielly Grigorievitch Tartakower

I like thinking big. If you're going to be thinking anything, you might as well think big.

Donald Trump

Surviving a failure gives you more self-confidence. Failures are great learning tools... but they must be kept to a minimum.

Jeffrey Immelt

To think is easy. To act is difficult. To act as one thinks is the most difficult.

Johann Wolfgang Von Goeth

Yesterday's home runs don't win today's games.

Babe Ruth

Personality Tests

I have found that it is much more important to hire a person with the personality than the best skills. This does not mean that you should not hire someone that has skills. I simply mean that skills can be learned while a personality cannot be changed. Also whenever you have two people applying for the same position with similar skillsets… always chose the better personality.

Some of this can be judged by your gut feeling. Hopefully if you're not the one doing the interviewing then the person that is doing it looks for the same things you're looking for.

I also found some awesome personality tests that you can give out to the potential employees.

Here's the link:

GRAB YOUR FREE RESOURCES HERE

buildabusinessbooks.com/freeresources

Please think about your legacy, because you're writing it every day.

Gary Vaynerchuck

Victory goes to the player who makes the next-to-last mistake.

Savielly Grigorievitch Tartakower

I like thinking big. If you're going to be thinking anything, you might as well think big.

Donald Trump

Surviving a failure gives you more self-confidence. Failures are great learning tools... but they must be kept to a minimum.

Jeffrey Immelt

To think is easy. To act is difficult. To act as one thinks is the most difficult.

Johann Wolfgang Von Goeth

Yesterday's home runs don't win today's games.

Babe Ruth

Payroll

Should you pay people yourself?

It depends.

There are two parts to this and a twist.

Writing a check to an employee or paying in cash is simple. That's part one.

Calculating all of the taxes and who gets them on what you just paid is not. This is when you would probably want some help. I've used a company called ADP before and they were good without being over-expensive. There are others so shop around. You submit the hours and amounts that the worker is getting and they take care of the rest.

Here's the twist.

Freelancers, Contractors or Outsourcers have to pay their own taxes and worry about that. You simply pay and mark down how much you paid in your expenses.

Average Salaries

Employees who are working in a convenient store are paid at $8.00 to $12.00 per hour depending on the type of store they are working in. The size of the store, where it is located and the number of years it has been in operation can also affect the income of the employee. Business owners on the other hand can earn around $45,000 yearly or more depending on the factors affeceting the business.

Job Ads

There are plenty of jobs that you can apply for within this business. Here are some examples of the job ads that you can find.

Convenience Store Manager - Higher Education - Boston University

Apply Now

Aramark (NYSE: ARMK) is in the customer service business across food, facilities and uniforms, wherever people work, learn, recover, and play. United by a passion to serve, our more than 270,000 employees deliver experiences that enrich and nourish the lives of millions of people in 22 countries around the world every day. Aramark is recognized among the Most Admired Companies by FORTUNE and the World's Most Ethical Companies by the Ethisphere Institute. Learn more at www.aramark.com or connect with us on Facebook and Twitter.

Responsibilities

About Higher Education

When it comes to on-campus dining, facilities services, sport arenas and conference center services, Aramark is the real head of the class. Partnering with close to 600 colleges and universities throughout the United States, we strive to provide the best residential, retail and catering options, service and facilities for students, faculty and administrator. Our programs are second to none in their innovation, excellence and results. As part of our commitment, we are determined to build and develop the best team of professionals in the industry - people who aren't afraid of spearheading change, who know how to lead and who appreciate endless opportunity.

Position Description:

Responsible for planning, directing and coordinating City Convenience Store activities in order to deliver a brand compliant high quality finished product to customers within the City Convenience Store and Subway within the store

Scope of Role:

Level of impact is a Convenience Store and Subway within the store. Manages 10 - 15 Aramark employees.

Key Responsibilities:

- Develop and be accountable for a safety culture that creates a work environment where no one gets hurt.
- Responsible for the operation of the entire convenience store and Subway deli.
- Establish & maintaining systems and procedures for the ordering, receiving, storing, preparing and serving of food & retail products.
- Ensure requirements for appropriate sanitation and safety levels in respective areas are met.
- Directly supervise employees with responsibility for hiring, coaching, performance management and reviews.
- Responsible for forecasting and accounting work.
- Conduct period inventory.
- Maintain records to comply with Aramark, government and accrediting agency standards.
- Coordinate activities with other internal departments and participates in management team meetings.
- Interface with vendors and key service users within client organization.
- Support all customer service and employee engagement initiatives.

Job Summary

Company
Josh Pliska

Location
Yuma, AZ 85364

Industries
Other/Not Classified

Job Type
* Full Time
* Employee

Career Level
Entry Level

Job Reference Code
00072255

Contact Information
* Josh Pliska
* Josh Pliska
* 796 S. 4th Ave
  Yuma, AZ 85364
* Phone: 9287836543

CONVENIENCE STORE CLERK Looking

About the Job

CONVENIENCE STORE CLERK

Looking for a self-motivated person. Job Duties consist of Restocking, operating a register, basic math skills, cleaning and organizing, customer service and interaction, propane sales, assisting customers with purchases, inventory, Tobacco and alcohol sales, Lottery and food preparation.

Clean background required. Must be able to work varied hours, stand for extended periods of time, lift (75lbs.), kneel, bend and climb.

Benefits: profit sharing and Health coverage.

Apply in person:
796 S. 4th AVE. MoNeece Mart Shell. 24 hour location, looking for all shift help.
(928) 783-8606

Yuma Sun Classifieds

50 | Page

Convenience Store/Bistro Associate

Brookdale Senior Living Inc.   Holland, MI 49423   10/18/2015

Apply Now

Part Time - varying hours 40:00am-8:00pm

Freedom Village Holland, MI 145 Columbia Avenue Holland, MI 49423

Job # 043979

A career with Brookdale has never been more rewarding! Brookdale is the only full-spectrum senior living solutions company and committed to providing the best options for all of the 110,000 residents we serve. The passion that we offer ensure residents continue to live the lives that they want while each meeting all of their needs along the way. Every day our dedicated associates to guarantee our promise is fulfilled in more than 1,150 communities in 47 states. Our Senior Living Solutions include: Independent Living, Assisted Living, Memory Care, Skilled Nursing, Continuing Care Retirement, Therapy, Hospice, Home Health, and Personalized Living.

More than a company; it is a calling.

Key responsibilities include:

* Completing inventories and properly displaying merchandise
* Assisting in purchasing of food and non-food items for the American Bistro
* Assisting in preparing fresh sandwiches from items that are available and operating in compliance data
* Assisting in serving meals as necessary on a timely basis
* Serving food in accordance with established portion control procedures and sanitation aid
* Assisting in daily or scheduled cleaning duties

We seek the following qualifications:

* High school diploma or GED

BROOKDALE
SENIOR LIVING SOLUTIONS
CAREERS

If you want a career that grows and not just a job, then you want to work at Brookdale.

Why?
As the largest provider of senior living solutions in the nation, your opportunities are almost unlimited. We have more than 80,000 associates devoted to providing exceptional service and care to our approximate 110,000 residents. As a result of our unparalleled service and outstanding reputation, we currently operate nearly 1,150 communities across 47 states and continue to grow.

We're always looking for passionate people to fill roles in operations, food service, marketing, human resources and resident care. We want those who are excited to use their expertise to enhance the quality of life for our residents. When you excel at your job, you enrich the lives of our residents.

At Brookdale, what you do matters every day.
It's not just a career, it's a calling.
Come be awesome with us.

For a complete listing of jobs, visit brookdalecareers.com

Systems

This is my favorite part and I can't recommend it enough to start building up systems from day one. A good rule is this: If you can do it and you do it often... and it makes you money than you shouldn't be doing it yourself.

If you do not take this advice then keep this in mind. You will spend a lot of time working in the business and not on the business. That's because you will be too tired to do so. You will also have a very hard time managing employees, scaling and finding new opportunities.

There are thousands of stories out there of people who set out to build a business in order to get money and freedom. Let's leave aside the startups that you see funded on Shark Tank by Venture Capital. Most of those will never make the owner money and an entire book could be written just on those. To sum it up though... in those types of businesses the founder is looking to make some revenue and grow (might never make profit) and sell to a bigger firm that wants them (either because their business can complement what the larger one is doing, they have an idea how to monetize it better or they want the competition gone).

Back to what you're building...

The business person quickly finds out that there is simply too much to do. He becomes responsive and becomes very reactive. The hours disappear and he can barely get his work done. The overwhelm and burnout hits him and he realizes that he does nothing more but work. Forget family and friends. Also the money is not there. Then a competitor comes and makes things even harder. Let's hope he doesn't go too much into debt. You get the picture.

On the other side of the coin you have a company like McDonalds that has amazing systems. Crappy food but amazing systems.

They know how to find a location. Almost every one of their franchises makes money if not all of them. They can train the new owner quickly. The employees do not need to possess any types of skills and can be replaced easily. Everyone knows their tasks, roles and exactly what is expected of them.

It's a much different experience running a business with systems than without.

I recommend some great books on this topic later on.

Helpful Podcast Episode:

LISTEN HERE

buildabusinessbooks.com/ep3

The golden rule for every business man is this: Put yourself in your customer's place.

Orison Swett Marden

To win without risk is to triumph without glory.

Pierre Corneille

People don't believe what you tell them. They rarely believe what you show them. They often believe what their friends tell them. They always believe what they tell themselves.

Seth Godin

A successful man is one who can lay a firm foundation with the bricks others have thrown at him.

David Brinkley

Instead of wondering when your next vacation is, you ought to set up a life you don't need to escape from.

Seth Godin

I had to make my own living and my own opportunity! But I made it! Don't sit down and wait for the opportunities to come. Get up and make them!

C.J. Walker

Productized Services

I want you to consider the following two scenarios very carefully:

Scenario #1 – A client comes in and asks for you to do a job. You ask them what they want and they start rattling off the different parts and components of the job. You do not want to lose them but know that this type of a custom job will take a lot of planning and be quite expensive. After all, someone has to pay the bills. You agree. After a while you figure that this is more complicated and harder than you previously thought. The couple of hours of research now turn into days and if you were honest with yourself and counted it all... you'd realize that you are starting to match the salary of a fast food worker. You call the client and say that it will take a bit longer and might cost more but they're pissed and don't want to hear it. You finish it, and hand it off to a now disgruntled customer while only making a couple of bucks.

Scenario #2 – A client comes and asks you to do some work for them. You show them a set menu list of the types of things you offer. It always starts with all the bells and whistles included but as they start objecting about money you simply look at them and say "what would you like for me to take off?" People hate losing things much more than they want to gain and so the customer huffs and puffs but takes almost everything. You know exactly how long it takes you to complete these jobs and the margins you have. Easy sale without much thinking involved.

That my friends is the difference between a custom job and a productized service. We have already spoken about systems in a previous chapter and let me ask you "which one do you think will be easier to scale and make money on?"

In order to get ready for Scenario #2 you will have to put in more work. You will have to complete the task and measure the time/cost/materials and write each stop down so that the next person can copy you. Don't worry. Nobody will steal your business from you… especially not your employee who would never withstand the responsibility of running the show. Even if they do… you can tweak the system, hire new people and leave them behind. This is the road to freedom.

The point here is to not have to think and re-shape the wheel for every customer. If you draw the line in the sand early on there won't be any whining/changing things/complaining later on.

Helpful Episode:

LISTEN HERE

buildabusinessbooks.com/ep4

People are best convinced by things they themselves discover.

Ben Franklin

I don't pay good wages because I have a lot of money; I have a lot of money because I pay good wages.

Robert Bosch

Opportunity is missed by most people because it is dressed in overalls and looks like work.

Thomas Edison

Everyone is a genius. But if you judge a fish by its ability to climb a tree, it will spend its whole life believing it is stupid

Einstein

Do or do not. There is no try.

Yoda

Your most unhappy customers are your greatest source of learning.

Bill Gates

Location

I assume you're already aware of this but location is everything. If you don't have foot traffic or eye balls that means that you have to find all of your customers. This is normal for large companies who set up offices somewhere in a cheap location and send sales people on the streets to hit offices door to door or have a team of cold callers.

You can do the sales yourself and there's nothing wrong with that but do not fall into the trap of making your first hire a sales person if you don't know how to sell anything yourself. It will destroy your business. That person will never care as much about your business as you do and will hold too much power over you.

Here is a list of tips to help:

- The city's zoning laws might allow for your kind of business in that area.

- The existing utilities should be up to code and adequate. Upgrading those on day one is not good.
- The lease/rent need to be reasonable. It's a part of your monthly overhead. Don't underestimate it.
- Employees are willing to come to your neighborhood. Hopefully you can find them right around the block because they live there. Safety and low crime rates are key.
- Also check insurance as it varies based on neighborhoods.
- Same with the customers. Rarely will someone drive out of their way to pay for anything. You're not the DMV, IRS, Welfare or an Immigration Office. They choose the worst locations on purpose.
- The area shouldn't depend on seasonal traffic. Vacation towns suck.
- Who is next door? Can you borrow their customers? Are they going to hang in for a while or are looking to run as soon as the lease is over? Introduce yourself and ask some questions. It's ok. They won't bite.

- We all drive cars. Look at the parking situation.

I prefer working from home, co-working spaces or coffee shops. It gives me more control over my time and location and most clients never know the difference. Also it creates a much smaller overhead and that money can stay in my wallet or go into the marketing budget.

Leadership is doing what is right when no one is watching.

George Van Valkenburg

In the business world, everyone is paid in two coins: cash and experience. Take the experience first; the cash will come later.

Harold Geneen

Those who say it can not be done, should not interrupt those doing it.

Chinese Proverb

Whatever the mind of man can conceive and believe, it can achieve. Thoughts are things! And powerful things at that, when mixed with definiteness of purpose, and burning desire, can be translated into riches.

Napoleon Hill

To succeed in business, to reach the top, an individual must know all it is possible to know about that business.

J. Paul Getty

A consultant is someone who takes the watch off your wrist and tells you the time.

Unknown

Healthcare

Here is how the Affordable Care Act (also called "Obamacare") impacts an average small business. For the sake of this discussion a small business has 25 or less employees. Anything above would be labeled as a "medium" or a "large" business.

You will need to:

1. Provide the employees with a notice that educates them about the Health Insurance Marketplaces. This will differ depending on the state. Inform that they might get a tax credit if purchasing their insurance through one of these marketplaces. Inform that they may decide to switch from the employer chosen insurance to the one of their choosing.
2. Increase Medicare withholding on the salaries. If you have read the other chapter you will know that I recommend for a 3rd company to take care of the payroll. These changes happen often and

it is simply too much to keep track of it and too easy to get in trouble by missing something.
3. The health insurance must be offered within 3 months of the employee joining. Previously some companies made the new hires wait longer until they could sign up for a company plan.

These rules apply to full time workers and is one of the reasons why so many corporations have been switching to part time workers, contractors and freelancers.

Further Reading: https://www.sba.gov/content/employers-with-fewer-25-employees

The only way around is through.

Robert Frost

The new source of power is not money in the hands of a few, but information in the hands of many.

John Naisbitt

The critical ingredient is getting off your butt and doing something. It's as simple as that. A lot of people have ideas, but there are few who decide to do something about them now. Not tomorrow. Not next week. But today. The true entrepreneur is a doer, not a dreamer.

Nolan Bushnell

You miss 100 percent of the shots you don't take

Jeffrey Immelt

Successful people are the ones who are breaking the rules.

Seth Godin

To the degree we're not living our dreams; our comfort zone has more control of us than we have over ourselves.

Peter McWilliams

Requirements

What do you need in order to open up your own convenience store? Investing in a convenient store can be profitable. In fact, if you wan to make a quick income, opening one can be very helpful. However you must first complete the requirements needed. Here are some of the important requirements that you should complete:

- Location is everything. A convenience store can be opened anywhere but if you have plans of one day franchising them, then you need a good location where people can easily spot it. Along the highway, downtown, or along gas stations are great spots for opening a convenience store. Once you have the location, contact your city realtor if it is available and secure it. You can either lease or purchase the location, either way both will work. If you cannot find a good place to open a convenience store, ask your realtor if they can help find one for you, this can also help.

- Check the permits you need from the county clerk's office and complete them. Register your business and have all the required business permits you need. Once you have it, you can start operating.

- Have a supplier that can provide you with the goods you need to sell. If you are going to sell alcohol, make sure that you have the permit to do so.

- Hire staffs for your convenient store. You can do the work but you also need to have some assistance. However if the convenient store you are planning to open is large, then you might have to hire a number of employees to do the work for you. Hiring security is also important as this could later help protect your business.

- Marketing is important for a business like this. You can use any kind of platform you like; you can advertise through newspapers, billboards, flyers or posters.

You can also make use of technology and build your own website for this. Signing up for a Facebook account, Twitter or Instagram is a good idea as well.

The absolute fundamental aim is to make money out of satisfying customers.

John Egan

If you would like to know the value of money, try to borrow some.

Benjamin Franklin

If it really was a no-brainer to make it on your own in business there'd be millions of no-brained, harebrained, and otherwise dubiously brained individuals quitting their day jobs and hanging out their own shingles. Nobody would be left to round out the workforce and execute the business plan.

Chinese Proverb

Get busy living or get busy dying.

from the "The Shawshank Redemption"

Winners take time to relish their work, knowing that scaling the mountain is what makes the view from the top so exhilarating.

Denis Waitley

Statistics suggest that when customers complain, business owners and managers ought to get excited about it. The complaining customer represents a huge opportunity for more business.

Zig Ziglar

Taxes

I predict a ton of interesting conversations that you will be having with your accountant but here's the one that comes up the most.

"I'm paying too much in taxes. The government is killing me here. What can I deduct or write of as a business expense?"

In the section I will list most of the 'legal' expenses that you can do. There's a reason I say this as you would be surprised some of the things that people try to write off.

Saying no to loud people gives you the resources to say yes to important opportunities.

Seth Godin

To think creatively, we must be able to look afresh at what we normally take for granted.

George Kneller

Business in a combination of War and sport.

Andre Maurois

To succeed... You need to find something to hold on to, something to motivate you, something to inspire you.

Tony Dorsett

Always forgive your enemies. Nothing annoys them more.

Oscar Wilde

All paid jobs absorb and degrade the mind.

Aristotle

Expenses

List of the most common expenses.

Turn the page.

Typical Business Expense Categories

Which ones will be applicable to your business?

- Accounting/bookkeeping, and financial consulting fees
- Advertising expenses
- Amortization
- Automobile expenses (only the percent that is used for business)
- Bad debts that you cannot collect
- Bank service charges and fees
- Board meetings
- Books and periodicals
- Building repairs and maintenance
- Business/trade conventions
- Business travel
- Business gifts (annual limit of $25 per recipient)
- Business meals (50% is deductible)
- Cafeteria health-insurance plan (requires plan)
- Charitable deductions made for a business purpose
- Cleaning/janitorial services
- Coaching fees, if related to your business
- Collection Expenses
- Commissions to outside parties
- Computer, printer, and software (if used over 50% for the business)
- Consultant fees
- Conventions and trade shows
- Costs of goods sold
- Credit card convenience fees

Typical Business Expense Categories

Which ones will be applicable to your business?

- Depreciation and amortization
- Discounts to customers
- Dues for professional and trade associations
- Education expenses for maintaining or improving required skills (Yourself & Employees)
- Email, Internet access, and web hosting services
- Employee wages
- Entertainment for customers and clients
- Equipment & repairs
- Exhibits for publicity
- Family member wages
- Fax machine
- Franchise fees (new)
- Freight of shipping costs
- Gifts for customers ($25 deduction limit for each) – recommend gift cards over cash
- Group insurance (if qualifying)
- Health insurance
- Home Office (not recommended)
- Insurance expense
- Interest
- Investment advice and fees
- Legal and attorney fees
- License fees and taxes

Typical Business Expense Categories

Which ones will be applicable to your business?

- Losses due to theft
- Management fees
- Materials
- Maintenance
- Merchant account or credit card processing fees
- Mortgage interest on business property
- Moving
- Newspapers and magazines
- Office furniture, fixtures and equipment
- Office supplies
- Online services used for the business
- Outside services
- Parking and tolls
- Payroll taxes for employees (Social Security, Medicare & Unemployment taxes)
- Parking and tolls
- Pension plans
- Postage and shipping
- Publicity
- Printing and duplication
- Prizes for contests
- Real estate – related expenses
- Rebates on sales
- Rent (business or during business travel)

Typical Business Expense Categories

Which ones will be applicable to your business?

- Research and development
- Retirement plans
- Royalties
- Safe-deposit box
- Safe
- Self-employment taxes
- Storage rental
- Subcontractors
- Start-up expenses (amortized over 60 months)
- State and local business taxes
- Preparation of business tax return
- Telephone expense (only for a separate business line)
- Travel expenses
- Utilities
- Website design
- Workers' compensation insurance

Audits

Here are the two main reason for getting the IRS to knock on your door and want to bend you over the table.

These are tips given to me by two different but amazing accountants.

1. Do not write off your home as a business expense. Things get very complicated here and usually throw up a red flag with the IRS. You will need to calculate the square feet used for business. How much time you spend there. The percentage of the utilities etc.
2. The IRS does not have a large work force and can only handle a small number of cases per year. What usually happens is that when they find someone that has been cheating on their taxes they will then go after the accountant who has completed that paperwork. It's not that this person will get in too much trouble

that should worry you but something bigger. Their book of business. This is what the government wants. It's a way for them to get a lot of easy wins which they love. Anytime you hear an accountant that is a little too creative walk away. You could be stepping on a land mine.

Winning is not a sometime thing; it's an all time thing. You don't win once in a while, you don't do things right once in a while, you do them right all the time. Winning is habit. Unfortunately, so is losing.

Vince Lombardi

There is no security on the earth, there is only opportunity.

General Douglas MacArthur

Never put off until tomorrow what you can avoid altogether.

Unknown

Hire character. Train skill.

Peter Schutz

For maximum attention, nothing beats a good mistake.

Unknown

Early to bed and early to rise probably indicates unskilled labor.

John Ciardi

Marketing

In order to market to a customer, it helps to know who that perfect customer is.

Few sample questions to ask yourself:

- How old are they?
- What are their interests?
- What's the gender?
- How educated are they?
- Do they have kids?
- Do they own a home?
- What kind of car do they drive?
- What is their average salary?

Answering these questions will give you a better idea of who this person is. Now you can go ahead and craft your message. The more in-tune you are the less your marketing budget needs to be.

Let me explain one more thing. There are two different types of marketing. One is to get a sale and the other is to build brand awareness.

Leave the brand building to the big companies for now. If you do have the budget for brand building... initially focus on one channel only.

For example: Local newspaper.

It will take weeks, if not months, of a person seeing your ad to even notice it. It will take even longer for them to become familiar with it and to start trusting it. After all you're starting to re-appear for a long time so you are not going anywhere. People like that. It will take even longer than that for them to actually remember you and call you. The process could take a year for each person. You never know when they start seeing your ad and whether they have a need for your service. Brand building is hard.

Not all advertising/marketing takes this long.

Here are some examples of marketing on a budget:

Flyers – These can be distributed around the area of your business or on a parking lot of a competitor. I'd say to keep it clean but you could potentially do that. Mailboxes or behind car windows make a good leaving spot. You can also hire a person to hand them out if you have a lot of foot traffic on the block.

Posters – Get them up in windows, on street corners or at the free advertising boards (such as the ones seen at entrances to most supermarkets or coffee shops). If you can offer something free to reel in the potential clients... even better.

Upsells – I already mentioned that it's a good idea to partner up with other businesses who sell similar products or services. Let me add to that. It is also great to have a free offer such as a consultation after which you can pitch your paid services. You might also have a tripwire which is a very low cost product that establishes trust between you and the customer making it easier to sell to them. It could be a trial offer (for a few dollars), a book or something else that you've seen others doing in your industry. Many of these are actually loss leaders. It's something worth more than you are selling it for but it hooks the person on wanting more of it from you. Bottom line is that these work great.

Referrals/word of mouth – Other businesses refer you. Customers refer you. This is something you will have to put some work in and build the right relationships. Also whatever you're selling needs to be good.

Follow-Up – Most companies drop the ball here. The sale is made and no one contacts the same customer again. There's a saying that your best future customer is your current customer. It costs much more to buy a new customer that it is to sell to a current one. It doesn't have to be the same offer.

Cold-Calling – This is my least favorite but it works. The problem with it is that you are throwing the net out very wide without a clue on who's around. It's a numbers game. Usually if you try and sell a 100 people something then one will end up buying it. Could be that they feel sorry for you but they will. If conversions are any lower than that, you are in trouble.

The Internet – Get me to the number one spot in Google and I will conquer the world. I've heard that one before. SEO takes a long time to work and is hard. It's unstable. It is a strategy that can break at any time. Google cannot be controlled and I like to think that it hates us. After all they make money through paid advertising only and not the free search. Look into ppc (pay per click) or at least combine it with SEO for quicker results.

It doesn't matter which of these methods you choose but it does matter that you measure the results. Stop doing things that do not work. I admit that having a show on YouTube is good for the ego but does it make you money?

Don't worry about people stealing your ideas. If your ideas are any good, you'll have to ram them down people's throats.

Howard Aiken

It takes more than capital to swing business. You've got to have the A. I. D. degree to get by ⸺ Advertising, Initiative, and Dynamics.

Ren Mulford Jr.

A calm sea does not make a skilled sailor.

Unknown

The worst part of success is to try to find someone who is happy for you.

Bette Midler

Your time is precious, so don't waste it living someone else's life.

Steve Jobs

Only when the tide goes out do you discover who's been swimming naked.

Warren Buffett

Networking

Networkign is an excellent way to make connections and find opportunities to make business with other people. When this is done correctly, networking can be very helpful to any business owner. If by case you are new to networking, it is important to know the dos and donts before you engage in and use this method. Here are a few things to remember.

Do:

- Find a good group to join in. Make sure that you join a group where in you can meet people who are also in the same niche as you are. It is important that you need to participate if you want to meet different kinds of clients.

- Place your best foot forward. This means that you have to do your best and be genuinely honest about what you do. Making up stories will not do you any good. An open and honest business owner is always a good introduction to do business, right?

- Create a good "sales pitch". If you have something to offer and if you are looking for clients or business partners in the future, all you need to do is create the perfect introduction of your services. It will also help you market your business.

- Have a goal to achieve. If you want to meet at least one person to do business with then by all means do so. Don't ever leave that event without reaching that goal. It would be a waste of time if you didn't.

- Make friends. The best way to make connection is to make friends during a networking event. This way it will be easy to make connections and find the right people to work with.

Don't:

- Don't be lazy when you are trying to mingle with people. This means you need to go around and be active when it comes to meeting people. Being lazy will get you nowhere.

- Don't give your business cards to everyone. Not everyone is there to do business or even try networking. So make sure that you choose those who you are giving your business cards otherwise you are just wasting them.

- Don't be afraid to ask questions. This is especially true if you are new to networking. Asking questions will give you more answers and lessons that you can apply to your business.

- Don't assume that everyone is there to do networking. It's best to be choose the people you are talking to. Not everyone is there to really do business, some are just there to socialize and nothing else. Be aware of who you are talking to.

- Don't be impatient as networking takes time. Make sure to nurture the relations that you have and results will come. Networking takes time so be patient.

Here's a link for further listening:

[LISTEN HERE](buildabusinessbooks.com/ep5)

buildabusinessbooks.com/ep5

Seminars & Conferences

http://www.cspnet.com/events

http://www.nacsonline.com/Pages/default.aspx

http://www.myappraisalinstitute.org/education/seminar_descrb/default.aspx?sem_nbr=OL-765&key_type=OOS

https://businessresources.peoples.com/SBR_template.cfm?Document=IndustryMarkets/retail-trade_shows.html

http://carreview2017.xyz/content/7-eleven-franchise-seminar

Linkedin Pages

https://www.linkedin.com/company/stripesconveniencestores

https://www.linkedin.com/company/vps-convenience-store-group

https://www.linkedin.com/company/convenience-store-decisions

https://www.linkedin.com/company/cefco-convenience-stores

https://www.linkedin.com/company/mac's-convenience-stores-inc-

Other Networking Opportunities

https://www.facebook.com/alldayconvenience store

https://www.facebook.com/Tlaamin-Convenience-Store-272244552956163/

https://www.facebook.com/chamsconvenience store

https://www.facebook.com/Ranglers-Convenience-Stores-Inc-125368164170062/

https://www.facebook.com/PakoConvenienceStore

https://www.facebook.com/XtraMart

Profit

If you can't make a profit you will go out of business. When looking at income reports on the internet from some of the more known marketers it's funny that they only speak about revenue. It means nothing. It's the same on the show called "The Profit". Many businesses that are making over a million in sales are still in debt. It's crazy.

Always focus on the bottom line.

One of the worst things to do is to sign up for a ton of monthly services. Carpet cleaning, SEO, forums, magazines etc...

These all look harmless individually but when grouped can really eat into what you will get to keep.

Another piece of the puzzle is the actual cost of production. Whether you're creating a physical product or performing a service it is crucial to understand the exact cost of it. Whether its supplies, electricity and/or time. They both c(money. If you do not have this part down then you cannot price things properly. It's impossible to have a healthy margin otherwise.

A margin is the difference between what you make the product for and what you sell it for. It's the money that you pay for your overhead and that you get to keep.

The overhead would be things such as the building, utilities not used for production, other employees, insurance etc…

It's also a good idea to break down your overhead into daily chunks. That way you know exactly how much you need to make per day to not go into debt.

Further Watching:

WATCH HERE

cnbc.com/live-tv/the-profit

Your income is directly related to your philosophy, NOT the economy.

Jim Rohn

The NBA is never just a business. It's always business. It's always personal. All good businesses are personal. The best businesses are very personal.

Mark Cuban

Fire the committee. No great website in history has been conceived of by more than three people. Not one. This is a deal breaker.

Seth Godin

Once you free yourself from the need for perfect acceptance, it's a lot easier to launch work that matters.

Seth Godin

You have brains in your head. You have feet in your shoes. You can steer yourself, any direction you choose.

Dr. Seuss

It is not the strongest of the species that survive, nor the most intelligent, but the one most responsive to change.

Charles Darwin

Margins

On the next couple of pages you will find the average profit margins broken down by each industry.

Industry	Number of Firms	Net Margin
Advertising	52	3.98%
Aerospace/Defense	93	7.64%
Air Transport	22	9.32%
Apparel	64	7.46%
Auto & Truck	22	3.16%
Auto Parts	75	3.44%
Bank (Money Center)	13	18.9%
Banks (Regional)	676	22.23%
Beverage (Alcoholic)	22	14.21%
Beverage (Soft)	46	12.66%
Broadcasting	28	11.56%
Brokerage & Investment Banking	46	12.48%
Building Materials	39	4.09%
Business & Consumer Services	177	4.29%

Industry	Number of Firms	Net Margin
Cable TV	18	9.31%
Chemical (Basic)	46	5.98%
Chemical (Diversified)	10	7.43%
Chemical (Specialty)	103	10.01%
Coal & Related Energy	42	-4.44%
Computer Services	119	5.56%
Computers/Peripherals	64	13.69%
Construction Supplies	55	6.14%
Diversified	23	10.12%
Drugs (Biotechnology)	400	11.18%
Drugs (Pharmaceutical)	151	15.95%
Education	42	1.99%
Electrical Equipment	126	5.64%
Electronics (Consumer & Office)	28	3.56%

Industry	Number of Firms	Net Margin
Electronics (General)	189	6.18%
Engineering/Construction	56	1.56%
Entertainment	84	12.59%
Environmental & Waste Services	103	3.08%
Farming/Agriculture	37	3.33%
Financial Svcs. (Non-bank & Insurance)	288	34.14%
Food Processing	96	6.87%
Food Wholesalers	14	1.79%
Furn/Home Furnishings	27	3.98%
Green & Renewable Energy	26	0.36%
Healthcare Products	261	9.49%
Healthcare Support Services	138	2.16%
Heathcare Information and Technology	127	6.72%

Industry	Number of Firms	Net Margin
Homebuilding	35	6.82%
Hospitals/Healthcare Facilities	56	4.50%
Hotel/Gaming	80	3.72%
Household Products	135	8.99%
Information Services	67	13.78%
Insurance (General)	24	8.47%
Insurance (Life)	25	8.19%
Insurance (Prop/Cas.)	52	9.00%
Investments & Asset Management	148	19.11%
Machinery	137	8.54%
Metals & Mining	124	1.63%
Office Equipment & Services	25	4.47%
Oil/Gas (Integrated)	8	9.99%
Oil/Gas (Production and Exploration)	392	7.52%

Industry	Number of Firms	Net Margin
Oil/Gas Distribution	85	3.04%
Oilfield Svcs/Equip.	161	3.81%
Packaging & Container	26	4.90%
Paper/Forest Products	22	2.58%
Power	82	8.03%
Precious Metals	147	-13.91%
Publshing & Newspapers	43	13.54%
R.E.I.T.	213	19.01%
Real Estate (Development)	18	1.26%
Real Estate (General/Diversified)	11	34.38%
Real Estate (Operations & Services)	52	4.96%
Recreation	68	8.69%
Reinsurance	4	8.52%
Restaurant/Dining	79	9.40%

Industry	Number of Firms	Net Margin
Retail (Automotive)	30	3.12%
Retail (Building Supply)	5	6.00%
Retail (Distributors)	90	4.23%
Retail (General)	23	2.67%
Retail (Grocery and Food)	21	2.71%
Retail (Online)	46	2.34%
Retail (Special Lines)	128	3.46%
Rubber & Tires	4	3.16%
Semiconductor	100	13.70%
Semiconductor Equip	47	4.73%
Shipbuilding & Marine	14	13.96%
Shoe	13	8.95%
Software (Entertainment)	20	10.11%
Software (Internet)	327	15.57%

Industry	Number of Firms	Net Margin
Software (System & Application)	259	17.34%
Steel	40	-4.33%
Telecom (Wireless)	21	-2.93%
Telecom. Equipment	126	14.51%
Telecom. Services	77	11.47%
Tobacco	20	22.42%
Transportation	21	4.96%
Transportation (Railroads)	10	18.29%
Trucking	30	3.78%
Unclassified	8	-43.05%
Utility (General)	21	8.71%
Utility (Water)	19	15.03%
Total Market	7887	7.84%

Public Relations

PR basically means free advertising.

Imagine that you just bought a newspaper. On one page you see an article on a new company that is very inspiring and doing thing differently in your town/city. They might be treating the employees differently, paying higher wages, and giving longer vacation or allow its people to work from home/coffee shops or abroad. You flip a few more pages and you see a huge ad. This one shows that there is a sale at a flower shop. There's a few word and a nice picture but you barely think of it and move on. Later on there is another article but it says paid advertising on the bottom or top. It talks about the benefits of a new supplement. The article is very dry and you get bored after one paragraph.

The difference here is that the first one cost that business nothing while the other two were paid for and were most likely not cheap. Getting a full page or two in any newspaper is not cheap.

Also most of us have a case of ad blindness and no longer respond well to them. It takes a lot of impressions (times the person views an ad) before they even realize it.

Where the first article could be stuck in your mind because you had an open mind while reading it.

Hiring a PR firm might not be in your budget or worth it. However contacting the local news does make sense if you have something to talk about. Remember that all of them need constant things to talk about.

Helpful podcast episode:

LISTEN HERE

buildabusinessbooks.com/ep6

The golden rule for every business man is this: Put yourself in your customer's place.

Orison Swett Marden

To win without risk is to triumph without glory.

Pierre Corneille

People don't believe what you tell them. They rarely believe what you show them. They often believe what their friends tell them. They always believe what they tell themselves.

Seth Godin

A successful man is one who can lay a firm foundation with the bricks others have thrown at him.

David Brinkley

Instead of wondering when your next vacation is, you ought to set up a life you don't need to escape from.

Seth Godin

I had to make my own living and my own opportunity! But I made it! Don't sit down and wait for the opportunities to come. Get up and make them!

C.J. Walker

Customer Management

There's no better client than the one you already have paying the bills. You need to keep track of them, continually communicate with them and keep them happy.

Here's a great episode on how to do this:

LISTEN HERE

buildabusinessbooks.com/ep7

It also touches on upselling and the tools to use for customer retention management. It also gives some great insights into what you need in place first before even trying to set up a system from which you can manage your existing clients.

The only place success comes before work is in the dictionary.

Vidal Sassoon

Speak the truth, but leave immediately after.

Unknown

The important thing is not being afraid to take a chance. Remember, the greatest failure is to not try. Once you find something you love to do, be the best at doing it.

Debbi Fields

Are you a serial idea-starting person? The goal is to be an idea-shipping person

Seth Godin

The problem with the rat race is that even if you win, you're still a rat.

Lilly Tomlin

Success in business requires training and discipline and hard work. But if you're not frightened by these things, the opportunities are just as great today as they ever were.

David Rockefeller

Additional Resources

I'm continually researching and compiling lists of the best available apps/habits/tricks/tips and anything else I can find on how to level up and grow as a person and how to expand my business.

This could be articles/links/books/videos/movies etc... (I don't discriminate)

You can get the most current version of that list here: FREE RESOURCES

buildabusinessbooks.com/freeresources

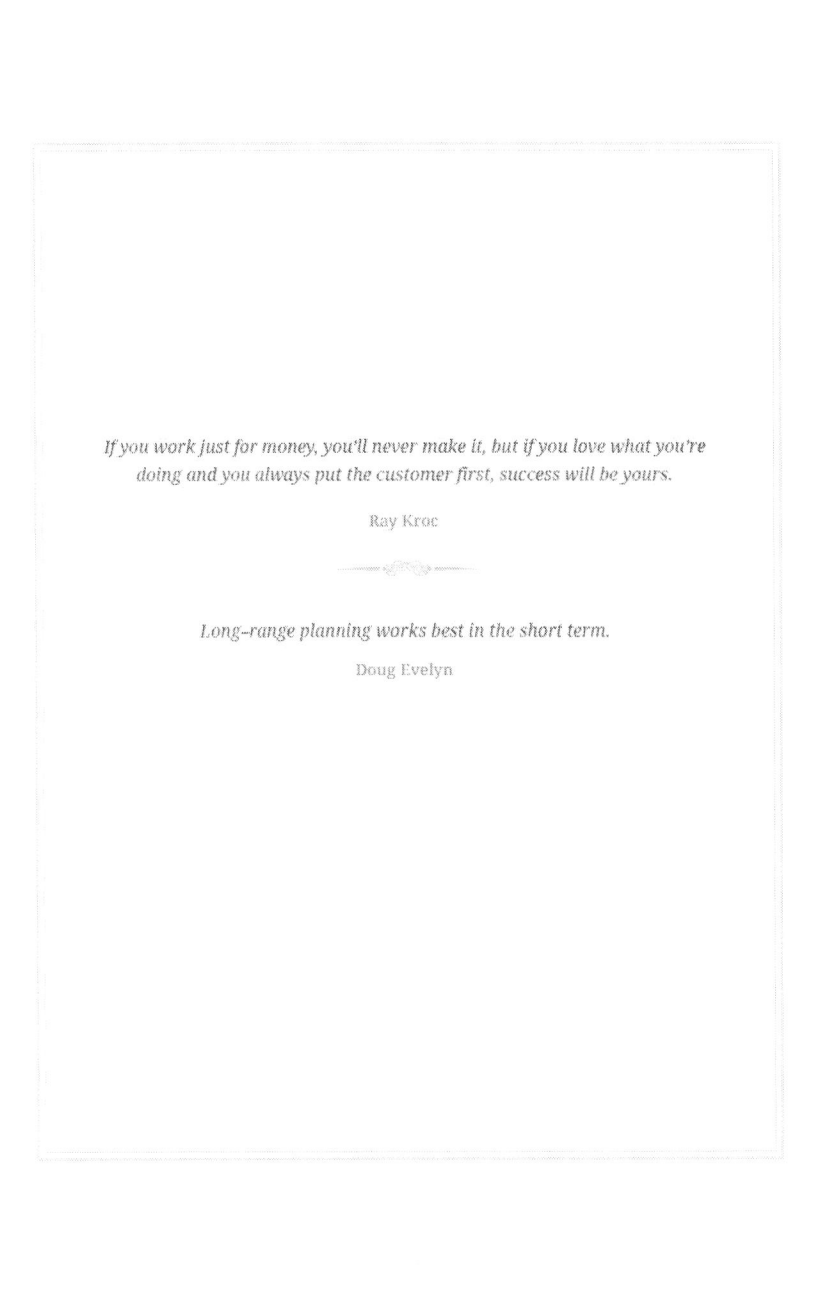

If you work just for money, you'll never make it, but if you love what you're doing and you always put the customer first, success will be yours.

Ray Kroc

Long-range planning works best in the short term.

Doug Evelyn

MASTERMINDS

This is the closest to a silver bullet or magic sauce that you will get to. One of the ways that I've seen businesses grown faster and smarter is when the owner joins a Mastermind.

A mastermind is a group of people from a similar field and with different levels of experience that meet on a regular basis and help each other grow. This is not a referral swap, meetup with a bunch of people trying to sell each other something or some other pyramid scheme. We've all attended plenty of those so do not get confused.

The point of the meeting is to address the problems that each member is dealing with at that exact moment. New walls crop up all of the time as we grow. When we're in the middle of the battle it is nice to get advice from someone that is looking at it from a hill above. Each person has a couple of minutes to explain what they are struggling with and the rest of the group gives suggestions or advice. The process can take 15-20 minutes or the entire mastermind.

I've seen it work both ways. Each person gets their problem solved or each week the group goes in-depth into someone's business.

Another huge component of this is the accountability. Not only do we have others around that understand what we are going through but after we commit to an action… during the next meeting the group will question us about it.

The last benefit and most likely the biggest is the friendships formed. Your network can grow very quickly through these types of masterminds. Unfortunately it's not that easy to form new ones and some do get stale after a while. Best ones consist of people from different industries so that you can get completely fresh insights and with people that you don't previously know.

The guys that created the movie "Your Own Way Out" came out with a very interesting idea and I was able to work out a deal with them.

(The movie shows an entire movement of people who are writing their own scripts and regaining freedom while growing their networks and businesses. It's very cool.)

They are organizing rotating masterminds. This means that every few weeks you join a new group. This gives a ton of eyeballs a shot at your business problems. Your network grows on steroids and the groups never get boring or old.

The offer can be found here: www.yourownwayout.com/special-books-offer/

SPECIAL DISCOUNT CODE: WINNER-N8

Leave a Review to Win a Kindle

[Click Here to Win a Kindle](buildabusinessbooks.com/review)

buildabusinessbooks.com/review

Made in the USA
Middletown, DE
26 July 2016